I Can Tell Time
with a Rhyme!

Tracy Kompelien

Consulting Editors, Diane Craig, M.A./Reading Specialist
and Susan Kosel, M.A. Education

ABDO
Publishing Company

Published by ABDO Publishing Company, 4940 Viking Drive, Edina, Minnesota 55435.

Printed in the United States.

Credits
Edited by: Pam Price
Curriculum Coordinator: Nancy Tuminelly
Cover and Interior Design and Production: Mighty Media
Photo Credits: ShutterStock, Wewerka Photography

Library of Congress Cataloging-in-Publication Data

Kompelien, Tracy, 1975-
    I can tell time with a rhyme! / Tracy Kompelien
      p. cm. -- (Math made fun)
    ISBN 10 1-59928-525-8 (hardcover)
    ISBN 10 1-59928-526-6 (paperback)

    ISBN 13 978-1-59928-525-2 (hardcover)
    ISBN 13 978-1-59928-526-9 (paperback)
    1. Time--Juvenile literature. 2. Time perception--Juvenile literature. I. Title. II. Series.

QB209.5.K664 2007
529--dc22

                                                                                        2006012562

SandCastle Level: Transitional

SandCastle™ books are created by a professional team of educators, reading specialists, and content developers around five essential components—phonemic awareness, phonics, vocabulary, text comprehension, and fluency—to assist young readers as they develop reading skills and strategies and increase their general knowledge. All books are written, reviewed, and leveled for guided reading, early reading intervention, and Accelerated Reader® programs for use in shared, guided, and independent reading and writing activities to support a balanced approach to literacy instruction. The SandCastle™ series has four levels that correspond to early literacy development. The levels help teachers and parents select appropriate books for young readers.

Emerging Readers	**Beginning Readers**	**Transitional Readers**	**Fluent Readers**
(no flags)	(1 flag)	(2 flags)	(3 flags)

These levels are meant only as a guide. All levels are subject to change.

We use clocks to
tell time.

Words used
to tell time:

a.m.
hour
midnight
minute
noon
p.m.

The hour hand
is the shortest hand.
There are 24 hours in
a day. The hour hand
goes around the
clock two times
each day.

This hour hand is pointing to the number three. I know that the hour is three o'clock.

The minute hand is longer than the hour hand. There are 60 minutes in an hour. The minute hand goes around the clock one time each hour.

The minute hand is pointing to the 5th line after the 12. I know it is five minutes after three o'clock, or 3:05.

What time is it? I know it is **10** a.m. **because it is before** noon.

The hours between 12 o'clock during the night (midnight) and 12 o'clock during the day (noon) are the a.m. hours.

What time is it? I know it is 1:00 p.m. because it is after noon.

The hours between 12 o'clock during the day (noon) and 12 o'clock during the night (midnight) are the p.m. hours.

I Can Tell Time with a Rhyme!

At in the morning,

Steve's gives a

warning.

By  his breakfast

is done.

He likes and eats

more than one.

fourteen

14

At 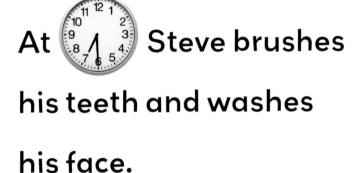 Steve brushes his teeth and washes his face. The comes in 15 minutes, so he needs to race!

Telling Time Every Day!

I wake up at 8 a.m. every morning.

I know that it is 8:00 a.m. because it is before noon. The sun rises in the a.m. hours.

eighteen
18

I go to school at
9:15 a.m.

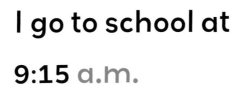

It is 15 minutes after nine o'clock. Another way to say this is quarter past nine.

twenty
20

I have soccer practice at 3:30 p.m.

It is 30 minutes after three o'clock. This is also called half past three.

twenty-two

22

I go to bed at 7:45 p.m. every night.

It is 45 minutes after seven o'clock. This is sometimes called quarter to eight.

Glossary

a.m. – short for *ante meridiem*, which is Latin for before noon.

half past – being a half hour, or 30 minutes, after the start of an hour.

p.m. – short for *post meridiem*, which is Latin for after noon.

quarter past – being a quarter hour, or 15 minutes, after the start of an hour.

quarter to – being a quarter hour, or 15 minutes, before the start of an hour.